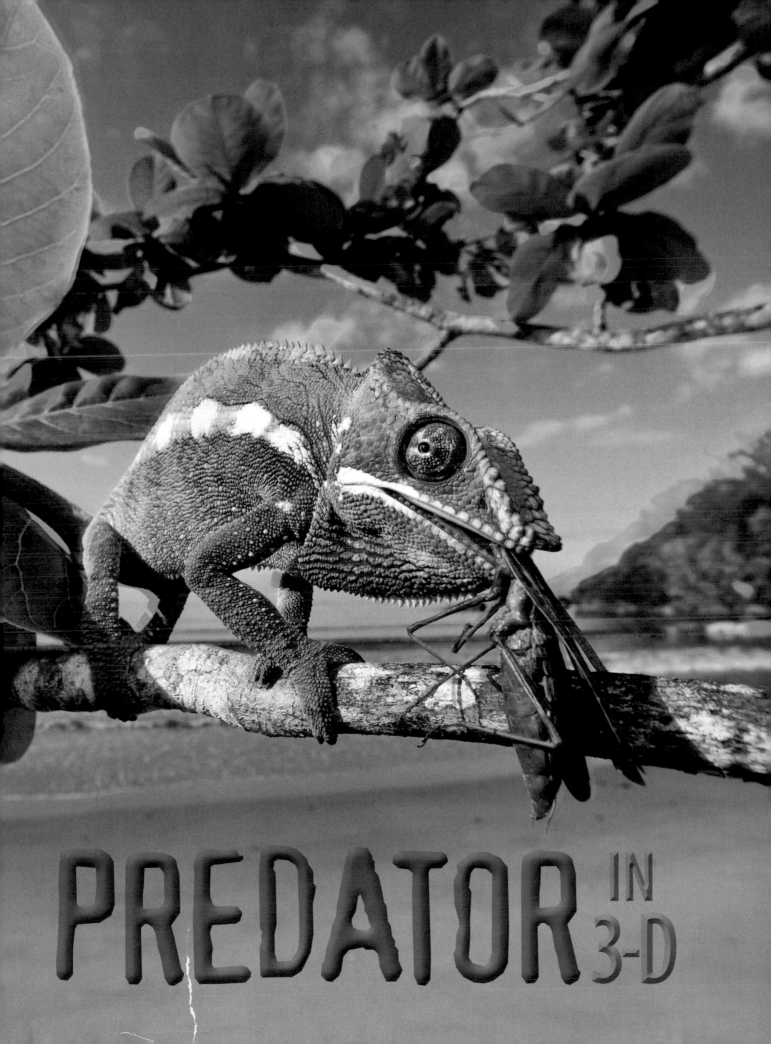

PREDATOR IN 3-D

DK

LONDON, NEW YORK, MELBOURNE,
MUNICH, AND DELHI

Written by John Woodward
Consultant Dr. Kim Bryan

Senior editor Ben Morgan
Senior art editor Smiljka Surla
Editor Sam Priddy
Assistant editor Damilare Olugbode
US editor Margaret Parrish
Designer Riccie Janus
Assistant designer Anna Reinbold
Picture research Nic Dean
Production editor Joanna Byrne
Production controller Angela Graef
Managing editor Julie Ferris
Managing art editor Owen Peyton Jones
Publisher Sarah Larter
Associate publishing director Liz Wheeler
Art director Phil Ormerod
Publishing director Jonathan Metcalf

First published in the United States in 2012 by DK Publishing
375 Hudson Street, New York, New York 10014

Copyright © 2012 Dorling Kindersley Limited
12 13 14 15 16   10 9 8 7 6 5 4 3 2
007—182437—Apr/12

A catalog record for this book
is available from the Library of Congress.
ISBN 978-0-7566-9021-2
Printed and bound in China by Hung Hing

Discover more at
www.dk.com

CONTENTS

WHAT IS A PREDATOR?

A PREDATOR is an animal that hunts and kills other animals (called prey) for food. Hunting live animals is far more difficult than eating plants, so predators need special skills and cunning strategies to survive.

Huge jaws lined with stabbing teeth are the main weapons of crocodiles.

TRICKS AND TRAPS

Some predators chase after prey, but others are more devious. Spiders build traps, and angler fish lure prey to their doom by making a fake worm appear to wriggle. Many predators are ambush hunters—they hide and wait for prey to come close and then launch a surprise attack.

Garden spiders build webs to capture flying Insects from the air.

LETHAL WEAPONS

Most predators aim to kill their victim quickly—otherwise, the captive might escape or fight back and injure the captor. To ensure a swift death, predators have lethal weapons such as razor-sharp teeth or claws. Some use chemical weapons: deadly venoms injected with fangs or stings.

JOINING FORCES

Most predators hunt alone, but a few hunters attack as a group. Lions and wild dogs hunt in organized teams, a strategy that helps them overpower animals too big to kill alone. Army ants raid the jungle in a swarm of millions, and piranhas attack in a frenzied, unorganized mob.

A wildebeest is no match for a whole pride of lions.

GREAT WHITE SHARK
TOP OCEAN PREDATOR

The eyes roll back into the head when the shark bites. They have internal reflectors for vision in poor light.

Nostrils draw water to sensitive scent detectors. The shark can smell prey from more than half a mile (1 km) away.

The ears can detect faint, low-pitched sounds from distant prey. They also aid the shark's sense of direction.

THE ATTACK

1 Detection
The hunt begins when a shark catches scent of a seal in the water. The shark turns and swims along the scent trail.

2 Charge
Some sharks circle prey, but the great white charges straight in with a burst of speed. The seal is knocked right out of the water.

3 Bite
The jaws snap shut on impact, and a sideways jerk of the head causes the razor-sharp teeth to slice through flesh with a sawing action.

THE GREAT WHITE SHARK'S SENSE OF SMELL IS GOOD ENOUGH T

THE GREAT WHITE SHARK
is the biggest of the killer sharks
and also one of the fastest. It is
equipped with a whole battery of
prey sensors and armed with a set
of teeth that can rip through
its victims like a chainsaw.

BUILT TO KILL

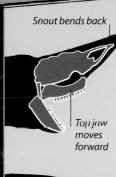

Snout bends back

Top jaw moves forward

Jaws snap shut

Jaws of death
A shark's jaw bones are separate from its skull. This allows the snout to bend out of the way when the mouth opens, while the jaws push forward ready to bite. As the jaws close they pull backward, yanking the victim into the shark's mouth and snapping shut with 20 times more force than a human's bite. Like steak knives, the 200 or so teeth have sawtooth edges for carving through flesh.

ACTUAL SIZE

Sawtooth edge

An enormous gape allows the great white to seize large prey and tear out a huge chunk of flesh in one bite.

SHOULD YOU BE SCARED?

! DANGER

Great whites kill more people than any other shark, but fatal attacks on humans are very rare. Only 134 deaths have been recorded worldwide. Most victims are bitten once and then abandoned, suggesting the shark mistook them for its normal prey but didn't like the taste.

Seen from below, surfers might be mistaken for dolphins or seals.

DETECT A SINGLE DROPLET OF BLOOD IN AN OLYMPIC-SIZED SWIMMING POOL.

All teeth and muscle, a great white shark bursts through a shoal of fish in the Pacific. A young great white would attack the fish, but older sharks like this one prefer sea mammals such as dolphins and seals.

CONSTRICTORS are large, powerful snakes that coil around prey and then tighten their grip until the animal dies of suffocation or a heart attack. The snake then swallows the body whole.

The African rock python is one of the largest constrictors and grows to 20 ft (6 m) long.

The snake's mouth can stretch open to an enormous size, allowing it to swallow prey far larger than its own head.

CONSTRICTOR
A SNAKE WITH A CRUSHING GRIP

SWALLOWING PREY

1 Finding the head
Snakes usually swallow prey headfirst so the animal doesn't get stuck in the throat. This corn snake is about to swallow a mouse.

2 Mouth expands
The bones in the snake's lower jaw are separate, allowing its mouth to stretch like elastic. The scales in its skin pull apart.

3 Into the stomach
The snake "walks" the sides of its mouth forward alternately, using backward-pointing teeth to haul the mouse into its throat.

THE WORLD'S LARGEST SNAKE—THE RETICULATED PYTHON—IS A CONSTRICTOR.

The central part of the snake's body is still coiled tightly around the impala's body after crushing it.

This impala is so large that the python will not need to eat again for many weeks.

BUILT TO KILL

Death by constriction

Some constrictors hunt by lying in wait to ambush prey, but others track down victims by following their scent. When the target animal is in range, the snake suddenly lunges to seize it in its sharp teeth and then quickly throws a few coils around it. Each time the animal breathes out, the snake tightens its grip like a noose so it cannot breathe in again. The snake's grip is so tight that the pressure can stop the victim's heart. Failing that, the animal soon dies of suffocation. Like other snakes, constrictors swallow prey whole and have special jawbones that separate to let the mouth open wide.

SHOULD YOU BE SCARED?

DANGER

Constrictors don't have venom, and all but the very biggest snakes are unable to eat adult humans because their mouths get stuck at the person's shoulders after swallowing the head. Nevertheless, constrictors can injure people with their teeth and they do occasionally kill people by constriction.

This 17-foot- (5.3-m-) long green anaconda was caught in Venezuela.

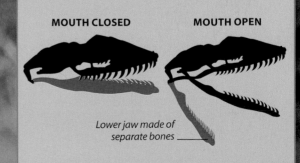

MOUTH CLOSED   MOUTH OPEN

Lower jaw made of separate bones

THE TIGER is the largest of the big cats and one of the most powerful predators on Earth. A solitary prowler, it relies on camouflage and stealth to creep close to victims and uses massive strength to overpower prey as big as buffalo.

The eye has a reflective layer in the back for better sensitivity at night. Vision is a tiger's primary hunting sense.

SHOULD YOU BE SCARED?

Although tigers are wary of humans and very rarely enter towns or villages, they do occasionally hunt and kill people who enter their territory. In the Sundarbans Forest of Asia, tigers kill 50–250 people a year. Tigers that have consumed human flesh can become regular man-eaters. One famous man-eater killed more than 400 people in Nepal and India before being shot in 1911.

DANGER

Stripes are an effective form of camouflage. In dappled shade or tall grass, tigers become almost invisible.

ONLY ONE IN 20 TIGER HUNTS IS SUCCESSFUL.

Muscle power

Tigers rely on sheer strength and physical bulk to pull down animals up to six times heavier than they are. Large prey are killed swiftly by strangulation, but small animals are killed in an instant by a bite so powerful it snaps the spine. Some tigers have been seen to kill prey with a blow from a paw so forceful that it smashed the victim's skull.

THE ATTACK

1 Stalk
Hidden by the long grass, the tiger creeps silently toward its target. It must get within 65 ft (20 m) without being seen or heard.

2 Pounce
The tiger charges from behind the animal, leaps onto it, and throws one paw over the prey's shoulder while it seizes its throat in its jaws.

Whiskers are sensitive to touch. They help tigers sense where to bite prey, in addition to helping them feel their way in the dark.

FACT FILE

Size: Up to 10 ft (3 m) long

Top speed: 40 mph (65 kph) in a short sprint

Main weapons: Teeth, claws, and muscle

Prey: Any medium-sized or large animals

Attack style: Stalk and charge followed by a lethal throttle

3 Throttle
The prey falls to the ground, but the tiger keeps a tight grip on its throat until it dies of strangulation. The victim's head is twisted to keep antlers out of the way.

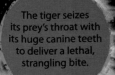

The tiger seizes its prey's throat with its huge canine teeth to deliver a lethal, strangling bite.

POLAR BEAR
ARCTIC HUNTER

THE POLAR BEAR is the only bear that eats almost nothing but flesh. It preys on seals on the drifting Arctic Ocean pack ice, attacking them as they surface to breathe, or ripping their defenseless pups from dens hidden under the snow.

THE ATTACK

1 Smash and grab
Ringed seals hide with their pups in snow caves, but a polar bear can sniff them out and smash through the roof to grab them.

The polar bear has an amazing sense of smell. It can detect a seal buried under snow from more than half a mile (1 km) away.

The narrow snout contains bladelike teeth for slicing flesh—very unlike the chewing teeth of other bears.

POLAR BEARS ARE EXCELLENT SWIMMERS, ABLE TO SWIM STEADIL

2 Death blow
The bear uses her strong claws to haul up the doomed seal and kills it with a single blow of her enormous paw.

3 Strip and share
The bear strips the skin and fat from the lifeless seal and shares it with her cubs. Any leftovers are gobbled up by scavenging birds.

Although it appears white, a polar bear's fur is actually transparent. It reflects light in the same way that snow does.

BUILT TO KILL

Grand slam
With a weight of up to 1,300 lb (600 kg), a polar bear is vastly bigger and heavier than its prey, and one swipe of its massive paw is enough to smash the skull of an adult seal. During the spring breeding season, the bear gorges on seal meat and fat to prepare for summer, when it may go without food for weeks after the sea ice melts.

A polar bear's sharp claws can tear a person's face off.

Big feet help to spread the bear's considerable weight on thin ice and act as paddles when swimming.

SHOULD YOU BE SCARED?

Polar bears are extremely dangerous, especially if they are hungry—as they often are when melting sea ice stops them from hunting normally. A polar bear will kill and eat a human if it can. Luckily, the human population of the Arctic is incredibly small, so casualties are rare, but the risk is very real.

A hungry polar bear will not hesitate to attack.

! DANGER

THE SALMON RUN

Every fall, Pacific salmon swim up Alaska's rivers by the thousand to breed—and grizzly bears wait to swat them out of the water with their huge paws. The bears fatten up on salmon in preparation for the long northern winter.

THE CHEETAH relies on speed to catch its prey. The fastest land animal on Earth, it can accelerate from 0 to 60 mph (0 to 100 kph) in three seconds and can outrun the swiftest antelope. Every aspect of its body is fine-tuned to maximize its racing ability.

Spots act as camouflage, concealing the cheetah as it creeps up on its prey.

The sleek but strong body is very slim, with no unnecessary weight to slow it down.

The deep chest contains big lungs to gather as much oxygen as possible—vital to power the muscles needed for running.

The legs are long and slender to maximize the length of the stride.

FACT FILE

Size: Up to 7½ ft (2.3 m) long (including tail)

Top speed: 60 mph (100 kph)

Main weapons: Large canine teeth and strong jaw

Prey: Mostly small antelopes such as gazelles

Attack style: High-speed chase followed by a choking bite to the throat.

THE CHEETAH CAN ACCELERATE AT THE SAME RATE AS A FORMULA 1 RACE CAR.

THE ATTACK

1 The chase
The cheetah creeps as close to a Thomson's gazelle as possible without being seen. It then launches its high-speed charging attack from behind.

2 In for the kill
The cheetah brings the animal down by striking its hind legs to make it trip. Before the prey gets back on its feet, the cheetah leaps for the throat.

3 Lethal bite
A powerful bite to the throat kills the victim quickly by suffocation. The cheetah rests briefly to cool down and then starts to eat.

The tail acts like a rudder, swinging to help keep the cheetah balanced in tight turns.

ATHLETE'S FOOT
Although the cheetah can retract its claws like other cats, they don't pull back into protective sheaths. This means that the claws are always exposed. They act like the spikes on an athlete's running shoes, improving the cheetah's grip and acceleration. Running on the claws wears their tips and makes them blunt, so the cheetah cannot use them to climb trees or seize prey.

BUILT TO KILL

Footwork
The cheetah has much the same running style as a greyhound dog. It throws its back feet forward to pass the front feet and then pushes them hard against the ground while stretching its front feet forward. This launches it into the air, giving it a huge, 22-ft- (7-m-) long stride at top speed. Its highly flexible spine can flex both ways, adding a spring to its step that also helps lengthen the stride.

Spine bends in an arch…

… and then bends the other way.

Stride length

KINGFISHER
HIGH-SPEED PLUNGE-DIVER

Transparent lids flip over the eyes during the dive to protect them from objects floating in the water.

The long bill has sharp edges so the bird keeps a secure grip on slippery, struggling fish as it flies back to its perch.

FACT FILE

Size: Up to 7 in (17 cm) long

Top speed: 60 mph (100 kph) when diving

Main weapons: Long, sharp daggerlike bill

Prey: Small fish, plus newts, tadpoles, shrimp, and aquatic insects

Attack style: Plunge-dives into water from a perch or from hovering flight

THE KINGFISHER can be easy to miss, since it perches quietly on a branch overhanging a river or lake, watching for prey. But when it spots a likely victim it explodes into action, hurling itself into the water in a streak of dazzling, electric blue.

A KINGFISHER MUST EAT AT LEAST ITS OWN BODY WEIGHT IN FISH EACH DAY.

The kingfisher must flap its wings powerfully when in the water in order to swim back to the surface.

FAST FOOD

Nesting kingfishers must catch as many as 2,500 fish to raise a family of up to eight hungry chicks—and when the young leave home, the pair raise another brood. They nest in a deep tunnel in the riverbank, which soon gets fouled with smelly fish remains and bird droppings.

BUILT TO KILL

Daggerlike bill

With its big head, long bill, tiny feet, and very short tail, a kingfisher looks awkward and top-heavy—but it is perfectly adapted for its hunting technique. Its long, daggerlike bill pierces the water so cleanly that the bird slips deep into the river with maximum speed and minimum splash, giving it the best possible chance of catching fast-swimming fish by surprise.

After catching a fish, the kingfisher beats its victim's head agains a branch to kill it.

THE ATTACK

1 Perch
From its perch on an overhanging tree branch, a kingfisher watches the river below for any sign of prey, such as a juicy fish.

2 Dive
When it spots a likely target, it picks its moment and drops forward off its perch, plunging straight down into the water.

3 Catch
It seizes the fish in its bill, rolls over, and uses its wings to power up to the surface, bursting back into the air in a flurry of spray.

IT SWALLOWS FISH HEADFIRST SO THE SCALES DON'T STICK IN ITS THROAT.

DRAGONFLIES are the falcons of the insect world—superfast aerial hunters that chase airborne insects at high speed and seize them in flight. They first appeared some 300 million years ago and are still masters of the air today.

The big, bulging eyes are made of hundreds of separate lenses and are especially sensitive to movement.

Sharp jaws are powerful enough to slice through the armored bodies of other insects.

DRAGONFLY NYMPH
Dragonflies spend the first stage of their lives living under water as nymphs. The nymphs are just as fearsome as the adults.

1 Watch
A dragonfly nymph watches as a fish swims within range of its secret weapon—an extending jaw with pincers at the tip.

2 Seize
In a flash, the nymph shoots out its jaw (known as its mask) to seize its victim. Impaled by the sharp pincers, the fish is helpless.

3 Devour
The voracious insect will devour every scrap of the fish. It lives like this for many months before turning into a flying adult.

DRAGONFLY
AGILE AIRBORNE PREDATOR

SOME DRAGONFLIES HUNT BY SNATCHING SPIDERS OUT OF THEIR WEBS.

The two pairs of long, transparent wings are reinforced with a network of rigid struts.

FACT FILE

Size: Wingspan up to 7½ in (19 cm)

Top speed: 36 mph (58 kph)

Main weapons: Fly-trapping legs and razor-sharp jaws

Prey: Mosquitoes, flies, bees, wasps, and other flying insects

Hunting strategy: Aerial ambush or pursuit

AERIAL ACROBAT

Dragonflies can flap their two pairs of wings independently, which gives them amazing agility in the air. They can make 90-degree turns, stop still, hover, fly backward, and dart forward in a blur of speed.

BUILT TO KILL

Body segments slant to keep legs forward

Bristly legs trap prey

Death grip

The dragonfly's legs are positioned under its head, where they are ideally placed for grabbing flies and passing them to the mouth. The legs are held in a cage shape during flight, allowing the dragonfly to scoop insects from the air. Long bristles on the legs stop prey slipping out.

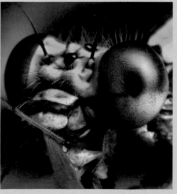

The huge eyes of dragonflies and their relatives the damselfies give superb all-around vision.

The bristly legs are used to scoop flying insects from the air.

OTHERS ARE POWERFUL ENOUGH TO CATCH AND EAT SMALL FROGS.

PEREGRINE FALCONS kill other birds in midair, ripping into them with their claws after diving into the attack at high speed. They can reach 185 mph (300 kph), making them the fastest animals on Earth.

Sharply pointed wings and large flight muscles in the chest make the peregrine a powerful flier.

1 Spot
The peregrine spots a pigeon from high above and begins a headlong dive, falling almost vertically with its wings closed.

The yellow feet end in large, piercing talons (claws) that are built to withstand the force of impact with the prey.

2 Dive
It accelerates to a blistering speed, giving the prey no chance to outpace it. The peregrine's wings begin to open as it steers toward the target.

Killer claw

PEREGRINE FALCON
FASTEST ANIMAL ON THE PLANET

BUILT TO KILL

Butcher bill
Birds of prey butcher their victims by holding the body down with the claws and tearing flesh with their hooked bill. The peregrine has an extra notch in its bill that helps it shear through neck bones to cut the spinal cord—a quick way of finishing off a victim that isn't yet dead. Then it uses the tip of the bill to rip away feathers and skin to get at the flesh. It often ignores the wings and feet, but strips everything else to the bone.

FACT FILE

Size: Up to 1½ ft (0.5 m) long

Top speed: 185 mph (300 kph)

Main weapons: Claws and hooked bill

Prey: Pigeons, crows, ducks, and seabirds

Attack style: Dives from a height or flies up from a perch to attack from below

SPIRALING HIGH

Like many other birds of prey, the peregrine can soar high into the sky with little effort by riding on updrafts of warm air called thermals. With wings outstretched, it circles lazily in the rising air, watching for prey.

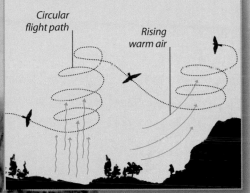

Circular flight path

Rising warm air

The large, dark eyes have fantastically sharp vision, allowing the peregrine to see six times farther than humans can.

Spreading the tail fan and wings helps the peregrine to brake after its high-speed dive.

3 **Approach**
Closing in from behind, the peregrine reaches out with a special, extra-powerful "killer claw," which can slice into the victim like a can opener.

4 **Strike**
The peregrine smashes into the pigeon and rips its body open. Fatally wounded, the pigeon drops to the ground, where the peregrine will eat it.

AND DIVE OFF THEM TO ATTACK PIGEONS IN THE STREETS.

SNATCHED BY AN OSPREY
The osprey hunts by swooping over lakes and plunging feetfirst into the water to snatch fish in its claws. This remarkable feat demands superb vision, great strength, and perfect timing.

THE AFRICAN WILD DOG is notorious for its ferocity. A highly efficient pack hunter, it relies on teamwork to bring down prey that is often larger than itself—which it then rips apart in gruesome fashion.

Long-distance runner

African wild dogs are built for the chase. They have terrific stamina and can run for many miles without tiring, doggedly pursuing a victim until it is exhausted. Like most predators, they select weak animals, and to make their choice they use a simple trick: get the herd running and then pick out a straggler and lock onto it.

AFRICAN WILD DOG
PACK HUNTER OF AFRICAN PLAINS

With a shorter muzzle than other dog species, the wild dog's jaw muscles exert more powerful leverage, helping it grip struggling prey.

FACT FILE

Size: Up to 5 ft (1.5 m) long

Top speed: 35 mph (60 kph)

Main weapons: Powerful jaws and meat-slicing teeth

Prey: Gazelles, antelope, and zebras

Attack style: Long chase followed by group attack

With long, slender legs and a lightweight frame, the wild dog is built for long-distance running.

NEARLY 80 PERCENT OF WILD DOG HUNTS END IN A KILL.

THE ATTACK

1 Grab
After a long chase, one dog grabs the prey by the lip, stopping it in its tracks. The rest attack from behind.

2 Kill
In a frenzy of activity, the whole pack falls on the animal and rips it to pieces while it is still alive.

3 Devour
The dogs wolf down the meat. Although the attack looks gruesome, the victim dies very quickly from massive blood loss.

The large ears give the animals excellent hearing and catch the breeze when the dogs are running, helping them keep cool.

The pattern of blotches is unique to each dog and provides camouflage in woodland surroundings.

MORTAL COMBAT

Wild dogs hunt the same prey as hyenas and lions and often end up in deadly fights with them. A pack of dogs can drive off a hyena, but they are no match for lions, which sometimes kill the whole pack—including cubs.

African army ants (driver ants) are blind and use their antennae (feelers) to follow scent trails and find their way around.

SHOULD YOU BE SCARED?

DANGER

Army ant soldiers have fearsome jaws that can give you a nasty nip. Fortunately, the army moves so slowly that it's very easy for people to get out of the way. Only people who are unable to move, such as babies or the sick, are in deadly danger.

The ant has a brushlike tongue that it uses to lap up food after chewing with its sharp jaws.

ARMY ANTS swarm through tropical forests like rivers of death, eating any animal that cannot escape their slicing jaws. Some of these murderous colonies contain as many as 20 million ants, all controlled by a single queen.

INSTEAD OF USING STITCHES TO CLOSE WOUNDS, NATIVE RAINFOREST PEOPLE

FACT FILE

Size: Soldier ants can be almost ½ in (10 mm) long

Top speed: Army progresses at 65 ft (20 m) per hour

Main weapons: Powerful jaws and sheer numbers. Some species have stings

Prey: Insects, spiders, and any other animals they can overwhelm

Attack style: Mass biting, eating prey alive

This soldier ant has huge, toothed jaws. Soldiers defend the rest of the colony from attack.

MOVING HOME

Army ants wreak such havoc in the forest that they cannot stay in one place for long. Every few days they must move their home to a new camp, taking their young with them.

These Asian army ants are carrying pupae that will hatch into adults.

THE ATTACK

1 Camp
Most types of army ant don't make permanent nests. Instead, they make temporary camps called bivouacs by linking their bodies together.

2 March
Each morning, the ants swarm out across the forest floor in long columns to search for food, protected by heavy-jawed soldiers.

3 Slaughter
Any animal that cannot escape is torn apart by hundreds of pairs of tiny sharp jaws, and the pieces are carried back to the bivouac.

OLD ARMY ANTS ON THEIR SKIN SO THE ANTS' JAWS CLAMP THE WOUND SHUT.

The line running along the flank of the fish is a special sense organ that can detect other animals in the water.

BUILT TO KILL

Razor teeth

With its blunt snout and bulky body, a piranha doesn't look like a killer. But when it opens its mouth it displays a fearsome set of triangular, razor-edged teeth. Normally piranhas use these for scavenging the remains of dead animals, but the clues that lead them to dying animals can also attract them to an injured animal with a minor wound. And then they just eat it alive.

The tail has powerful muscles that drive the fish rapidly through the water as it charges into the attack.

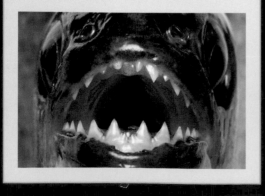

A PIRANHA school can detect the slightest trace of blood in the water and as the scent grows stronger it triggers a feeding frenzy. The fish hurl themselves into a mob attack, tearing every scrap of flesh from their victim and even killing and eating each other.

Big eyes see well in dim light and face slightly forward for 3-D vision, although visibility can be limited in murky rivers.

Large nasal pits contain highly tuned chemical sensors that can detect blood drifting in the water.

Powerful muscular jaws work fast to scissor flesh from bone, allowing the piranha to strip its victims with awesome speed.

FACT FILE

Size: Up to 12 in (30 cm) long

Top speed: 25 mph (40 kph) in short bursts

Main weapons: Razor-edged interlocking teeth

Prey: Animals from worms, insects, and small fish to large wounded mammals

Attack style: Uncoordinated mass attack and reckless feeding frenzy

THE ATTACK

1 Scent
The piranhas pick up the scent of blood from an animal in the water and gather like underwater vultures.

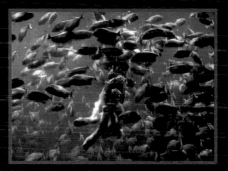

2 Feeding frenzy
They attack in a frenzy of excitement, slicing away the victim's flesh. As blood billows into the water, the fish go crazy, attacking each other.

3 Bare bones
Within minutes, the last shreds of meat have been devoured, leaving nothing but a bloody skeleton, and the surviving fish swim away.

SHOULD YOU BE SCARED?

DANGER

There are plenty of gruesome stories about people being set upon by bloodthirsty piranhas, but there is not much hard evidence to show that this happens. People get bitten, but not often. Even so, if you are ever in the Amazon rainforest, where piranhas live, never go swimming if you are bleeding. You wouldn't want to prove the stories right.

A luckless piranha victim meets a quick, bloody end.

By combining forces, these powerfully built animals can bring down prey as large as buffalo and giraffes.

Retractable claws stay very sharp so that they can be used as weapons to cling to animals and drag them down.

LION
AFRICA'S TOP PREDATOR

THE ATTACK

1 Stalk
A group of lionesses creep up on a buffalo herd from different directions, keeping low to stay hidden in the long savanna grass.

2 Charge
The first lioness springs up and charges at full throttle, but she makes her move too soon and her target manages to get away.

3 Ambush
It runs into the path of another lioness, which leaps onto it, sinking her claws in and dragging it sideways to the ground with her weight.

MALE LIONS ARE MUCH BIGGER THAN FEMALES BECAUSE THEIR ROLE IS T

Lions depend on their excellent vision for targeting prey, although scent is important when hunting at night.

SHOULD YOU BE SCARED?

DANGER

Some lions are man-eaters. People make easy targets, especially at night, and have always been at risk. But as wild grazing animals have become scarce, more and more lions have turned to human prey. Between 1990 and 2004, lions in Tanzania killed at least 563 people.

Most man-eaters are lone males who are forced to hunt solo.

FACT FILE

Size: Male up to 11 ft (3.4 m) long (including tail)

Top speed: 34 mph (55 kph)

Main weapons: Strength, sharp claws, stabbing canine teeth

Prey: Mainly large, hoofed mammals

Attack style: Stalk followed by short charge and throttling bite

Muscular legs are adapted for strength rather than speed, but lions can run fast in short bursts.

BUILT TO KILL

Extreme force

Like all cats, lions have short jaws with fewer teeth than the average carnivore. This enables the jaw muscles to exert maximum leverage on the massive, stabbing canine teeth, which a lion uses to kill its victims with a throttling bite. The lion's cheek teeth, called carnassials, have bladelike edges and work like scissors. Lions use them to slice through tough hide and to cut flesh from bones.

SKULL FROM SIDE

Jaw muscle attached here

Meat-slicing carnassial teeth

Long, stabbing canine teeth

FRONT VIEW

4 Kill
The lioness kills the buffalo by clamping her jaws on its throat to suffocate it. The others gather around and start to feed.

FATAL FOOTWORK
Big cats often bring down prey by striking a hind leg to make the animal lose its footing. This kudu was ambushed when it came to a waterhole to drink—the lion was waiting in hiding nearby.

THE RATTLESNAKE is a highly specialized predator of small mammals such as mice. It can track prey in total darkness, and it kills with a single bite, its fangs injecting a lethal dose of blood-destroying venom.

Camouflaged skin helps rattlesnakes to hide but also means that people often step on them by mistake.

BUILT TO KILL

Venomous fangs

Rattlesnakes have sharp fangs that inject venom. The fangs are very long so that venom is injected deep into the wound, and they are hinged at the base so they can fold back when the snake closes its mouth. On biting, muscles around the venom glands contract to squirt venom through the fangs. The venom causes intense pain and vomiting as it attacks the victim's blood and internal organs.

Fangs inject venom

Venom is stored in venom glands

THE ATTACK

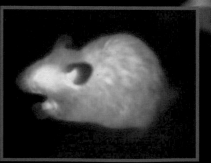

1 Scent
A rattlesnake picks up the scent of its prey using its forked tongue to sense chemical traces left by an animal on the ground.

2 Seek
It slithers into the animal's burrow and locates it in the dark, using heat-sensitive pits in its snout to form a crude image.

3 Attack
It strikes the animal with its fangs and waits for the deadly venom to take effect. The snake then swallows the body whole.

SCORPIONS AND BEES CAUSE FAR MORE HUMAN

WARNING RATTLE

The rattle forms from loose rings of skin that are left on the tail when the snake sheds its skin. When it feels threatened, the snake shakes its rattle as a warning to other animals to keep clear.

FACT FILE

Size: Up to 4 ft (1.2 m) long

Top speed: 3 mph (5 kph)

Main weapons: Fangs that inject a blood-destroying venom

Hunting strategy: Follows a scent trail using forked tongue, and targets prey with eyes and heat sensors

Prey: Mostly mice and birds

Large eyes give good vision in poor light. The pupils are vertical slits, a feature common among animals that hunt at night.

The forked tongue is a rattlesnake's main sense organ, used to pick up the scent of prey.

Heat sensors in special pits give the snake a kind of night vision, allowing it to see warm-blooded animals in pitch darkness.

SHOULD YOU BE SCARED?

! DANGER

Rattlesnake bites can kill, but if a person receives antivenom within two hours of being bitten, they have a 99 percent chance of surviving. Antivenom is made by collecting venom and injecting it into a sheep. The sheep's blood makes antibodies that destroy the venom, and the antibodies are then purified and stored.

Rattlesnakes are "milked" for venom by pushing the fangs into a test tube.

JELLYFISH
FLOATING DEATHTRAPS

JELLYFISH are among the simplest creatures on Earth, with no heads or brains and no internal organs. They swim lazily through the seas, snaring small creatures in stinging tentacles that inject a deadly venom. Some jellyfish are armed with so many stings that they can kill a person in only four minutes.

BUILT TO KILL

Micro stingers

The tentacles of a jellyfish are covered with thousands of stings that are too small to see with the naked eye. Each sting is stored within a cell. On top of the cell is a tiny hair that acts as a trigger. If a fish touches the trigger, the sting bursts out and its needle-sharp tip pierces the skin and injects a shot of venom. Fish that blunder into the tentacles of jellyfish are stung thousands of times, the venom paralyzing and killing them.

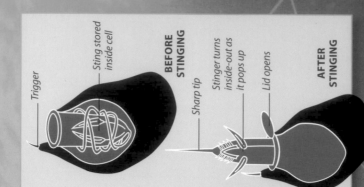

Trigger

Sting stored inside cell

BEFORE STINGING

Sharp tip

Stinger turns inside-out as it pops up

Lid opens

AFTER STINGING

Long, slender tentacles armed with stings hang from the body, ready to catch prey.

The bell-shaped body swells to take in water and then squeezes it out to push itself forward.

THE BOX JELLYFISH HAS 30 MILLION STINGS ON ITS TENTACLES.

FACT FILE

Size: The lion's mane jellyfish can reach up to 120 ft (37 m) in length (including its tentacles)

Top speed: Box jellyfish can swim at up to 3.4 mph (5.4 kph)

Main weapons: Stinging cells that inject venom

Prey: Small sea animals such as fish and shrimp

Attack style: Prey trapped in long stinging tentacles

SHOULD YOU BE SCARED?

DANGER

Most jellyfish are just a nuisance, but some are killers. The box jellyfish of Australia and Indonesia have killed dozens of people. Their venom contains a murderous cocktail of poisons. One poison destroys skin and flesh, causing agonizing pain and leaving scars that take months to heal. Others break down blood cells, paralyze nerves, and stop the heart.

Australian beaches affected by box jellyfish sometimes have danger signs.

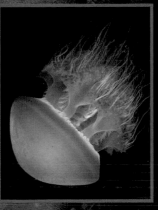

Stingless jellyfish
Some jellyfish have weak stings that have no effect on human skin. However, the stings still help the animals capture their prey.

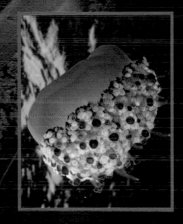

Fried egg jellyfish
This large yellow jellyfish preys on other jellyfish. Its tentacles are colored purple by tiny plantlike organisms living inside it.

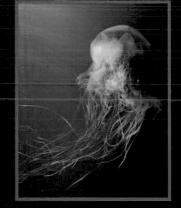

Lion's mane jellyfish
The largest jellyfish species, the lion's mane jellyfish can grow to longer than a blue whale, making it the longest animal in the world.

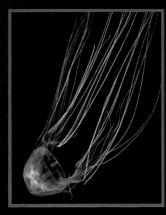

Box jellyfish
The deadly box jellyfish has a squarish body, with a cluster of venomous tentacles dangling from the four bottom corners.

THE SCORPION emerges at night to creep through the dark, its senses tingling for any trace of prey. When a victim is found, the scorpion seizes it with its claws and drives its sting into the prey's body, paralyzing it with venom before mashing it to a pulp.

GLOW IN THE DARK

Scorpion skin contains a fluorescent chemical that glows in ultraviolet light. No one knows why the chemical is there, but it helps scientists find scorpions in the dark.

Yellow scorpion
This scorpion species is common in Mediterranean countries. In North Africa, its venom is deadly, but European yellow scorpions merely cause a painful sting.

The tail can arch right over the scorpion's head to inject a lethal dose of venom.

Claws seize prey, which the scorpion mashes up with its jaws, using digestive juices to liquefy the flesh.

SCORPION
A STING IN THE TAIL

A SCORPION CAN SURVIVE ON JUST ONE INSECT A YEAR, AND IT NEVER NEEDS TO

BUILT TO KILL

Lethal injection

Scorpions are related to spiders, but instead of being armed with venomous fangs, a scorpion has a sting on the end of its long tail. Deadly venom is injected into a victim in order to paralyze it as quickly as possible. Small creatures are killed instantly.

Big venom glands

SCORPION TAIL

HITCHING A RIDE

Instead of laying eggs, female scorpions give birth to live babies. They are just like their parents, but are much smaller and have pale, soft skins. Their mother carries them for protection—although she may eat one or two if food is scarce.

Female scorpions carry babies on their backs.

Fat-tailed scorpion
The venom of this deadly scorpion, which is common in North Africa, contains nerve poisons that can kill a person within two hours.

Deathstalker
The deathstalker of Africa and the Middle East has the most deadly venom of all scorpions. More than half of children stung by it die.

Arizona bark scorpion
Far more dangerous than a rattlesnake, this scorpion killed at least 800 people in Mexico in the 1980s. Victims can suffer for up to 72 hours.

DRINK—IT GETS ALL THE MOISTURE IT NEEDS FROM THE JUICY FLESH OF ITS PREY.

A robberfly sucks the life out of a dragonfly it has captured in midair. Robberflies kidnap flying insects and stab them with their mouthparts to inject a deadly venom. The fatal injection also liquefies the victim's insides.

SELF-DEFENSE

A mantis is a killer, but that doesn't mean it's safe from attack by other predators. When threatened, a mantis tries to scare off its attacker by standing tall and spreading its arms and wings to appear bigger. Some flash bright colors at the same time in an attempt to startle their enemies into backing off.

FACT FILE

Size: Up to 6 in (15 cm) long

Main weapons: Trapping forelegs

Prey: Mainly insects and spiders, but large mantises can kill mice, birds, frogs, lizards, and even snakes.

Attack style: Ambushes prey from hiding and then decapitates it (cuts off its head) or eats it alive.

The forelegs are hinged like jackknives so they can extend and then snap shut around prey.

Spikes line the inside of the forelegs to trap struggling victims and prevent their escape.

With its head bitten off, this cricket makes an easy meal for the hungry mantis.

MANTIS
CAMOUFLAGED AMBUSH HUNTER

A MANTIS is a living trap. Beautifully camouflaged and heavily armed, this ambush predator sits still and waits for prey to come to it. It relies on virtual invisibility and split-second timing to snare victims in a deadly embrace.

MANTISES DON'T WAIT FOR VICTIMS TO DIE—THEY EAT THEM ALIVE.

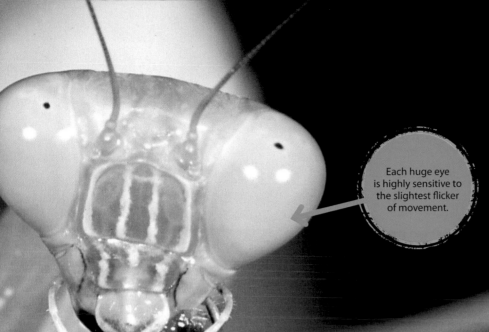

Each huge eye is highly sensitive to the slightest flicker of movement.

The mouth contains sharp jaws that scissor through tough insect prey with ruthless efficiency.

THE ATTACK

1 **Poised for action**
Perched almost motionless except for its head, the mantis watches intently as a fly lands within range of its trapping forelegs.

2 **Lightning attack**
In a fraction of a second, too fast for us to see, the mantis shoots out its long, wickedly barbed arms to snatch the fly from the twig.

3 **No escape**
Snared by the sharp spines, the fly is doomed. Within seconds, the mantis will shear off its head and settle down for a meal.

BUILT TO KILL

Camouflage
A typical mantis is brown or green to make it hard to see among leaves or grass. But some are pearly white or even pink, allowing them to hide in brightly colored flowers. They may also have broad flaps on their legs that resemble petals. These amazing creatures lie in wait in flowers, poised to snatch butterflies and bees that come to gather nectar.

This Malaysian orchid mantis is pink to match the petals of orchid flowers.

THE ORNATE HORNED FROG of South American rainforests relies on camouflage to conceal it on the forest floor as it waits to ambush prey. It will snatch any animal that comes close to its mouth—even if it's too big to swallow.

FACT FILE

Size: Up to 5 in (14 cm) long

Main weapons: Gigantic mouth

Prey: Other frogs, mice, small birds, snakes, and insects

Attack style: Sits still, waiting to ambush animals that wander past.

BUILT TO KILL

Big mouth

Most frogs pick up insects with a flick of their sticky tongues, but the horned frog grabs larger prey in its huge jaws, using the tongue to help scoop them up. As wide as its head, the mouth is equipped with powerful muscles to clamp it shut and toothlike spikes to trap prey. The frog's eyeballs pop down into its head as it swallows to help push the body down.

Mouth clamped shut

Mouse

Eyeballs pop in

Vision is the frog's most important sense. It it will only target moving prey.

FROG-EATING FROG

Most frogs and toads eat insects, spiders, and other small animals. The ornate horned frog, however, preys mainly on other frogs and toads. It will even eat smaller ornate horned frogs—including its own relatives, especially if it is kept as a pet in a confined space.

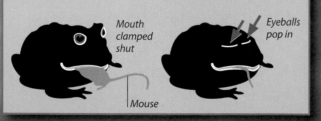

WHEN THREATENED, THE ORNATE HORNED FROG SWELLS UP AND SCREAMS.

THE ATTACK

1 Watch and wait
The frog sits and waits without moving, watching for a likely victim to stray within range. It may have to wait a long time.

2 Snatch
When a mouse wanders past, the frog leaps forward and snatches it. Trapped in the frog's vicelike jaws, the mouse is doomed.

3 Swallow
The frog swallows the mouse alive, retracting its eyeballs and using its front foot to help push the mouse down its throat.

The skin pattern looks decorative, but it provides vital camouflage when the frog is lying in ambush.

The horned frog's mouth is enormous, taking up about half of the body.

IT SOMETIMES SWALLOWS ANIMALS SO BIG THAT IT CHOKES ITSELF TO DEATH.

THE NILE CROCODILE is an ambush hunter that lurks unseen in African rivers, waiting to kill animals that come to the water. The nearest thing alive to *Tyrannosaurus*, this massive, flesh-eating reptile will slaughter and devour virtually any animal it comes across.

Plates of bone are embedded in a crocodile's skin, forming an incredibly tough, protective coat of armor.

The jaws contain 60–80 pointed teeth that sprout in ragged rows. They are replaced many times in a crocodile's life.

GOOD MOTHERS

Female crocodiles are very attentive parents. They lay their eggs on land, buried under sand or a mound of rotting leaves. When their eggs hatch, the mother helps the babies to dig their way out. Then she gently picks them up in her mouth and carries them to the water, where she will look after them for up to two years.

The eyes are high on the head so the crocodile can watch prey while its body is mostly hidden in the water.

CROCODILES HAVE EXISTED SINCE THE AGE OF THE DINOSAURS.

THE ATTACK

1 Approach
As zebras start to cross a river, watching crocodiles glide quietly toward them with only their eyes and snouts above the water.

2 Seize
With a powerful flick of its muscular tail, one of the crocodiles surges forward through the water and seizes a zebra's head with its jaws.

3 Drown
The crocodile drags its victim under water to drown it. Other crocodiles join in. They grab the body and spin around to tear it apart.

The crocodile grips the zebra with its teeth and then spins around violently in the water to tear off flesh.

BUILT TO KILL

Jaws of death
The crocodile's pointed teeth are good for gripping but they cannot chew or slice. So to tear prey into chunks that can be swallowed whole, the crocodile uses its body strength, gripping the animal and then rolling in the water. The jaws close with great force, but the muscles that open them are weak—you could hold a crocodile's mouth shut with your hands.

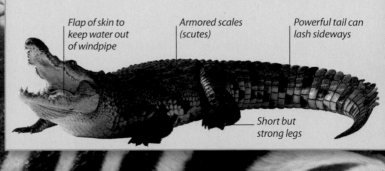

Flap of skin to keep water out of windpipe

Armored scales (scutes)

Powerful tail can lash sideways

Short but strong legs

NILE CROCODILES CAN LIVE FOR MORE THAN 100 YEARS.

CHAMELEONS are famous for their ability to change color, but they are also expert hunters. A chameleon captures insects by firing its elastic tongue like a missile and seizing victims with its sticky tip.

The tail can wrap around branches. This helps the chameleon anchor itself as it reaches forward to attack.

CHAMELEON
KILLS WITH A FLICK OF THE TONGUE

FIGHTING COLORS

Chameleons change color to show anger or attraction to other chameleons or to become camouflaged. The trick relies on tiny dots of color in the skin that can expand or shrink.

RUDIS CHAMELEONS FIGHTING

The toes are fused together to form two strong hooks opposite each other for gripping branches.

THE DWARF CHAMELEON IS THE WORLD'S SMALLEST CHAMELEON.

HE ATTACK

1 Aim
The chameleon spots grasshopper and creeps ery slowly forward, its eyes xed on the target. It takes im with its tongue.

2 Fire
Suddenly it shoots out its tongue, propelling the sticky tip toward its target with pinpoint accuracy and lightning speed.

3 Pull back
Gripped by the suction cup on the tongue's tip, the insect is helpless as the chameleon rapidly hauls it back into its mouth.

DWARF CHAMELEON (ACTUAL SIZE)

Chameleons can swivel their eyes to look in two different directions. During a hunt, both face forward for 3-D vision.

Like the tip of an elephant's trunk, the tip of a chameleon's tongue contains muscles that can grip objects.

Bone within tongue

BUILT TO KILL

Telescopic tongue

The chameleon's tongue is hollow and has a stiff but slippery bone in the middle. The soft, outer part of the tongue is stored scrunched up over the bone like a sleeve pulled up a person's arm. When the chameleon attacks, it flicks the bone forward out of its mouth. At the same time, muscles in the tongue contract to make it shoot forward at whipcrack speed, slipping off the bone as it goes.

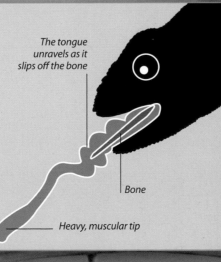

The tongue unravels as it slips off the bone

Bone

Heavy, muscular tip

WHEN ATTACKED, CHAMELEONS SWELL UP LIKE BALLOONS TO LOOK BIGGER.

THE KOMODO DRAGON of southern Indonesia is a true monster—a giant lizard powerful enough to kill and devour deer, buffalo, and even its own kind. An adult can swallow a goat whole and can eat up to 80 percent of its own body weight in a single meal.

Size: Up to 11 ft (3.3 m) lon

Top speed: 11 mph (18 kph

Main weapons:
Long claws and sharp, serrated teeth

Prey: Deer, pigs, goats, and reptiles—including smaller Komodo dragons

Attack style: Ambush and charge, attacking the vulnerable underside of the victim

SHOULD YOU BE SCARED?

! DANGER

Scientists think the Komodo dragon's saliva contains a dangerous venom.

To a Komodo dragon, a human being is just another tasty snack. Young children are particularly at risk—several are known to have been killed and eaten. The dragon might look docile, but it can move alarmingly quickly if it wants to, and its venomous bite can inflict horrific wounds.

KOMODO DRAGON
WORLD'S BIGGEST LIZARD

A KOMODO DRAGON DEVOURS EVERYTHING—SKIN, BONES, SKULL, AND EVEN HORNS.

Murderous weapons

A fully grown Komodo dragon can fell a deer with one blow of its powerful tail, and then hold it down with its long claws while it tears it apart with its ripsaw teeth. Even if its victim escapes, an anticlotting agent in the dragon's saliva ensures that the victim's wounds keep bleeding, and the dragon can follow it until it is too weak to defend itself.

Sharp claws

Short, strong legs

Flicking forked tongue

Long, muscular tail

FINDING PREY

1 **Following the scent**
Using its forked tongue to sample the air, a Komodo dragon can detect the scent of a dying animal from up to 6 miles (10 km) away.

2 **Taking a bite**
It latches onto its victim and pulls, wrenching its head sideways to rip through skin and tendons with its curved, steak-knife teeth.

3 **Others join in**
The smell of death soon attracts other dragons, which squabble over the spoils. The biggest either push the others aside or kill and eat them.

Watchful eyes see well by day and are very sensitive to movement. They do not work so well in the dark.

Waterproof, scaly skin stops the dragon from drying out in the tropical sun. The tough scales also act as armor.

The Komodo dragon has very weak jaws and relies on serrated teeth and strong neck muscles to tear apart its victims.

LATER IT VOMITS UP THE INDIGESTIBLE PARTS IN A DISGUSTING SMELLY LUMP.

Clinging to a branch with its muscular tail, an African Great Lakes bush viper lunges with its long fangs. Its venom destroys blood and flesh and is deadly to the small animals on which it preys.

HUMPBACK WHALE
TRAPS FISH IN A NET OF BUBBLES

THE HUMPBACK WHALE devours entire schools of small fish and other sea creatures. It can catch them by the thousand, thanks to its cavernous mouth and ingenious hunting tactics.

The whale's pointed upper jaw is smaller than its lower jaw and is studded with knobs called tubercles.

A curtain of bristles (baleen) in the whale's upper jaw works like a built-in fishing net.

BUILT TO KILL

Sifting the sea

Like many whales, the humpback feeds by taking a huge gulp of seawater into its immense mouth and then forcing it out though a curtain of bristles hanging from its upper jaw. The bristles, which are called baleen plates, act as a giant strainer, trapping fish and other animals in the whale's mouth. The whale often attacks from below, lunging up through a school with jaws agape.

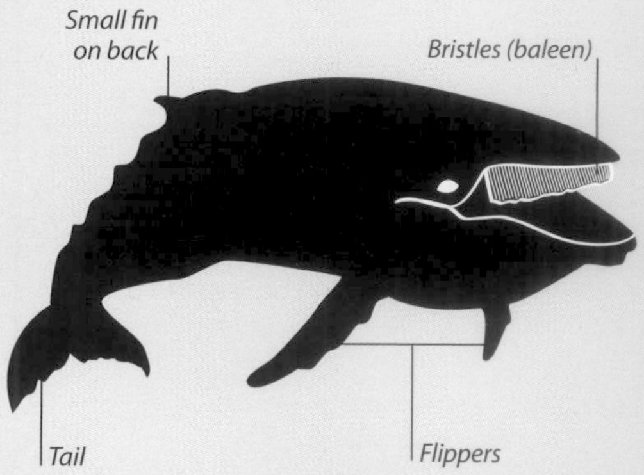

Bristles (baleen)

Small fin on back

Flippers

Tail

DESPITE ITS HUGE APPETITE, A HUMPBACK WHALE STOPS EATING IN

BREACHING

Humpbacks are famous for leaping from the water and falling back with a mighty splash, a habit known as breaching. Why they do this is unclear. It might help to dislodge barnacles on the skin or it could be a signal to other whales. Perhaps they do it just for fun.

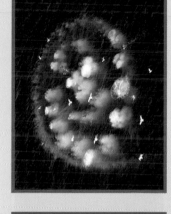

The enormous body is visible deep below the water. A humpback whale weighs as much as 600 people.

Pleats in the whale's throat allow it to expand like a balloon and hold a vast amount of water.

FACT FILE

Size: 39–52 ft (12–16 m) long

Top speed: 16 mph (26 kph)

Main weapons: Huge mouth

Prey: Fish and shrimplike animals called krill

Attack style: Swallows a whole school of fish, then squirts the water back out

THE ATTACK

1 Bubble net
Humpback whales often work together to herd fish into a tightly packed school by surrounding them with a "net" of bubbles.

2 Charge
With the fish trapped by the bubble net, the whales dive beneath them and start swimming straight up toward the surface.

3 Attack lunge
Each huge animal surges up through the water with its mouth wide open, to engulf up to a thousand fish in a single deadly lunge.

THE VENUS FLYTRAP is a predatory plant—a killer that catches and devours insects that land on its deathtrap leaves. After snapping shut to trap a victim, the leaves produce chemicals that dissolve the body, helping the plant obtain vital nutrients that it cannot get from the soil.

BUILT TO KILL

Hair trigger

Each half of a flytrap leaf is equipped with three tiny, stiff hairs that act as triggers. If a raindrop or a fleck of dirt falls on a hair, nothing happens. However, if an insect nudges a hair twice in quick succession or touches two hairs within 20 seconds, the trap snaps shut. It takes only a tenth of a second for the trap to close, sealing the insect's fate.

The gaps between the teeth allow small insects, which are not worth eating, to escape.

VENUS FLYTRAPS SOMETIMES CATCH AND CONSUME SMALL FROGS.

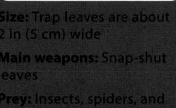
Size: Trap leaves are about 2 in (5 cm) wide

Main weapons: Snap-shut leaves

Prey: Insects, spiders, and other small animals

Attack style: Trapping

The trap consists of a special kind of leaf with spiked teeth. It folds in half to form a cage, trapping the insect inside.

THE ATTACK

1 Tempt
Insects and other small creatures are attracted by the plant's vivid red color and land on one of the flytrap's open leaves.

2 Trap
As the prey walks across the leaf, it disturbs the trigger hairs on the surface—the two halves of the flytrap snap together in a split second.

3 Devour
The plant's teeth interlock to form a cage so the victim cannot escape. The more it twitches, the tighter the trap squeezes shut.

The fly struggles to get out of the trap, but the plant's digestive juices have already begun to attack its body.

A STICKY END

The Venus flytrap is not the only flesh-eating plant. The leaves of the sundew plant are covered with hairs that secrete a sweet-tasting fluid that insects find delicious. But the fluid is as sticky as glue, and once an insects gets stuck, the leaf curls around it and kills it.

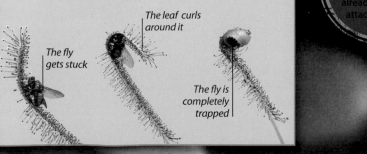

The leaf curls around it

The fly gets stuck

The fly is completely trapped

ANGLER FISH
DEEP-SEA PREDATOR

ANGLER FISH encourage their prey into danger by dangling a lure that looks temptingly edible. If another fish swims close to investigate, the angler suddenly opens its huge mouth so water rushes in, taking the fish with it.

A long spine sprouting from the fish's forehead carries a lure that the fish can twitch like a juicy worm.

The eyes are all but useless in the dark ocean depths. The fish relies on touch instead.

The huge, gaping mouth bristles with sharp, needlelike teeth. Once caught, prey have no chance of escape.

Long feelers growing out of the fins can sense the movement of other animals in the water.

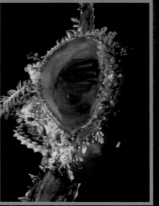

Monkfish
This shallow-sea fish spends most of its life lying on the seabed, dangling its lure and waiting for victims to swim into its ambush.

Hairy frogfish
The hairy frogfish lives in the coral seas of the tropical Indian and Pacific oceans, where its skin tassels help conceal it among the reefs.

THE ANGLER FISH'S STOMACH CAN EXPAND TO AN INCREDIBLE SIZE

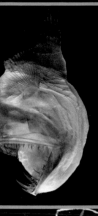

Humpback angler

This deepwater angler fish attracts its prey with a lure that glows in the dark. Its nightmarish teeth form a deadly trap.

Black seadevil

This angler fish lives in water as deep as 4,700 ft (1,430 m) and has a luminous lure. The male is tiny and lives attached to the giant female like a wart.

Hunting by feel

The bizarre fanfin angler fish is a deep-ocean predator that lurks far below the surface, using sensitive feelers to detect prey in the dark.

The big, elastic stomach can stretch to hold prey bigger than the angler's own body.

FACT FILE

Size: Up to 5½ ft (1.7 m) long, although small species are only 1½ in (3.5 cm) long

Main weapons: Tempting lure, huge mouth, and often very long, sharp teeth

Prey: Smaller fish, although some anglers can eat fish as big as themselves

Attack style: Ambush, using lure to tempt prey within range of huge mouth

HIDDEN TRAP

Angler fish that live on shallow seabeds rely on camouflage to conceal themselves from their prey. Each fish can change its skin color to match sandy, gravelly or weedy seabeds, and it flicks sand and shell fragments onto its back to add to the effect. Once settled, it lies motionless—except for its twitching, tempting lure.

The frilly tassels around this monkfish help it to hide on the seafloor.

When it sits on the sand, the tassels hide its outline and it seems to vanish.

FACT FILE

Size: Up to 10 in (25 cm) across (including legs)

Top speed: 1.2 mph (2 kph)

Main weapons: Venom-injecting fangs

Prey: Mainly insects, but some large tarantulas kill frogs and birds

Attack style: Capture prey with silk traps or actively hunt them, before killing with a venomous bite

SPIDERS hunt insects and other small animals, using venomous fangs to kill them before sucking out their insides. Many spiders make cunning traps from silk to detect and capture prey, but others are hunters, stalking and pouncing on victims just as cats do.

Jumping spiders hunt by sight and have eight eyes, two of which are huge. Other spiders rely more on touch than vision.

SHOULD YOU BE SCARED?

Nearly all spiders are armed with venom for killing prey. Most can't bite humans or don't inject enough venom to do serious harm. However, some spiders can cause nasty wounds, and Sydney funnel-web spiders, black widows, and Brazilian wandering spiders inject nerve toxins that can kill.

DANGER

The curved fangs are attached to hairy, armlike structures. Venom is pumped through the fangs.

Jumping spider
The tiny jumping spider slowly sneaks up on insects when they aren't watching. When close, it leaps on top of its victim and bites it to inject lethal venom with its fangs.

The black widow kills about six people a year in the US.

SPIDER
TRAP BUILDER

GRAM FOR GRAM, SPIDER SILK IS SIX TIMES STRONGER THAN STEEL WIRE.

Net-casting spider
This spider holds a silk net in its front legs. When an insect walks past, the spider stretches the net and throws it over the victim to trap it.

Labyrinth spider
Lurking in a funnel-shaped silken lair, this grassland spider waits for insect prey to get trapped in its horizontal, sheetlike web.

Trapdoor spider
Hidden beneath a hinged trapdoor, this powerful spider rushes out to seize insects that blunder into a network of silk tripwires.

All spiders have eight long legs, equipped with sensory bristles that detect vibrations, sound, and even scent.

BUILT TO KILL

Silk traps

Spiders are famous for building webs to trap their prey, using stretchy silk produced by glands in their rear. Garden spiders make beautiful spiral webs, but other spiders make webs that look like sheets, hammocks, or funnels. When an insect touches the web, the spider can feel the silk move through its feet and darts across the web to inject a paralyzing dose of venom. This digests the victim's flesh, turning it to a liquid that the spider can suck into its stomach.

Building a web

The spider spans a gap with strong silk and adds a Y-shaped frame.

Its adds more threads leading from the center to the outside.

The spider then works in a spiral, laying sticky silk around the frame.

Web makers such as garden spiders often wrap victims in silk to stop them from escaping.

THE WORLD'S DEADLIEST SPIDER IS THE BLACK WIDOW.

INDEX

ACKNOWLEDGMENTS

Dorling Kindersley would like to thank Jim Sharp at 3dimages for 3-D work and Chris Bernstein for the index.

The publisher would also like to thank the following for their kind permission to reproduce their photographs:
(Key: a-above; b-below/bottom c-center; f-far; l-left; r-right; t-top):

1 naturepl.com: Nick Garbutt (c). 2-3 Corbis: Mary Clark (c). 3 Corbis: Yann Arthus-Bertrand (br). 4-5 Photolibrary: Perrine Doug/Pacific Stock (c). 4 Corbis: Masa Ushioda/Specialist Stock (bl). naturepl.com: Juan Carlos Munoz (bc). SeaPics.com: C & M Fallows (br). 5 Alamy Images: Photo Resource Hawaii (br). 6-7 Corbis: David Fleetham/ Visuals Unlimited (c). 8-9 Photolibrary: Werner Bollmann/OSF (c). 8 Ardea: John Canacalosi (bc); John Cancalosi (br, bl). 9 NHPA/Photoshot: Tony Crocetta (bc). 10 Getty Images: Paul Chesley. 10-11 Corbis: Tom Brakefield (c). 11 Corbis: Tom Brakefield (cr). FLPA: Tim Fitzharris/Minden Pictures (tr); Terry Whittaker (br). Photolibrary: Mike Powles/OSF (tl). 12-13 Photolibrary: Gérard Lacz (tc). 12 NHPA/Photoshot: Jordi Bas Casas (tr). 13 FLPA: Rob Reijnen/Minden

Pictures (tc). naturepl.com: Steven Kazlowski (cr); Andy Rouse (c). NHPA/Photoshot: Jordi Bas Casas (tl). 14-15 Andy Rouse Wildlife Photography: Andy Rouse (c). 16-17 Photolibrary: Winfried Wisniewski/ Bridge (c). 17 Alamy Images: AfriPics (tl). FLPA: Suzi Eszterhas/Minden Pictures (c). Photolibrary: Michel & Christine Denis-Huot (tc); Fritz Polking/Peter Arnold Images (tr). 18-19 Photolibrary: Gisela Delpho/Picture Press (c). 19 Ardea: Zdenek Tunka (cb). FLPA: Reinhard Hölzl/Imagebroker (bl); Paul Sawer (cr). naturepl.com: Charlie Hamilton James (tr, br). 20 FLPA: Mitsuhiko Imamori/Minden Pictures (bl, bc, br). 20-21 FLPA: Jef Meul/ Foto Natura/Minden Pictures (tr). 21 Corbis: Tim Zurowski/All Canada Photos (cr). Thomas Shahan: (br). 22 Ardea: Jim Zipp (tl, c). NHPA/Photoshot: Richard Kuzminski (bc). 22-23 Ardea: Jim Zipp (c). 23 Adrian Dancy: (c). 24-25 FLPA: Scott Linstead (c). 26-27 Getty Images: Andy Rouse (c). 26 naturepl. com: Bruce Davidson (tr). 27 FLPA: Suzi Eszterhas/Minden Pictures (tc, tl, tr). naturepl.com: Christophe Courteau (br). 28-29 naturepl.com: Martin Dohrn (c). 28 naturepl.com: Martin Dohrn (c). 29 FLPA: Chien Lee/Minden Pictures (cb); Piotr Naskrecki/Minden Pictures (br).

naturepl.com: Martin Dohrn (tr, cr). 30-31 Photolibrary: Paulo de Oliveira/OSF (c). 30 Alamy Images: Amazon-Images (bl). 31 Getty Images: Raphael Gaillarde/ Gamma-Rapho (tr, cr, br). Photolibrary: Tony Allen/OSF (bc). 32-33 Photolibrary: Michel & Christine Denis-Huot (c). 32 FLPA: Peter Oxford/Minden Pictures (bc, br). naturepl.com: Peter Blackwell (bl). 33 FLPA: Peter Oxford/Minden Pictures (br). 34-35 Photolibrary: Martin Harvey/Peter Arnold Images (c). 36-37 Photolibrary: Radius Images. 36 Alamy Images: Cliff Keeler (bl). Getty Images: Bianca Lavies/National Geographic (br). Photolibrary: (c). Science Photo Library: Edward Kinsman (bc). 37 Ardea: John Cancalosi (br). NHPA/ Photoshot: Martin Harvey (tl). 38-39 Photolibrary: Mark Conlin/OSF (c). 39 Alamy Images: Poelzer Wolfgang (bl). Corbis: Jason Isley - Scubazoo/Science Faction (tr); Paul Souders (crb). SeaPics.com: Gary Bell (br). 40-41 Photolibrary: Christophe Véchot/Bios (c). 40 Getty Images: Albert Lleal/Minden Pictures (cl). 41 Ardea: John Cancalosi (br). Getty Images: Tim Flach (bl). Wikipedia: Ester Inbar (bc). 42-43 Thomas Shahan: (c). 44-45 Thomas Marent. 44 FLPA: Mitsuhiko Imamori/Minden Pictures (cl). 45 Getty Images: Barcroft Media (bc). 46-47 Science Photo Library: Jim Merli/Visuals Unlimited (c). 46 Alamy Images: Corbis Cusp (cb). Photolibrary: John Cancalosi (br).

48 Photolibrary: Mark MacEwen/ OSF (bl). 48-49 FLPA: David Tipling (c). 49 FLPA: Suzi Eszterhas/Minden Pictures (tr tl); David Tipling (tc). 50-51 NHPA/ Photoshot: Stephen Dalton (c). 50 Igor Siwanowicz: (cb). 51 Thomas Marent: (tl, tr). SuperStock: NHPA (c). 52-53 FLPA: Stephen Belcher (c). 52 Getty Images: Michael Dunning (cl). 53 FLPA: Mark Jones/ Minden Pictures (tr). naturepl.com: Michael Pitts (ca). Photolibrary: Fred Bruemmer (cr) Reinhard Dirscherl (br). 54-55 Ardea: Michel Menegon (c). 56-57 FLPA: Yva Momatiuk & John Eastcott/Minden Pictures. 57 Corbis: Specialist Stock (tr, cra, cr). Getty Images: Alexander Safonov (tr). 58-59 Ardea: Pat Morris (c). 58 Wikipedia: Noah Elhardt (cb). 60-61 naturepl.com: David Shale (c). 60 Photolibrary: Fredrik Ehrenstrom (tc). SeaPics.com: Jeff Rotman (tr). 61 FLPA: Norbert Wu/Minden Pictures (tl). SeaPics. com: Florian Graner (br); Doug Perrine (tc); Espen Rekdal (fbr). 62-63 Barcroft Media Ltd..: John Hallmen (c). 62 Corbis: Robin Loznak/Zumapress (bl). 63 naturepl. com: Nick Garbutt (tl); Hans Christoph Kappel (tr); Wild Wonders of Europe/Arndt (tc). Science Photo Library: Claude Nuridsany & Marie Perennou (bc)

All other images © Dorling Kindersley
For further information see:
www.dkimages.com